TABLE OF CONTENTS

2 Acknowledgements	116 Merchandise Mart
3 Table of Contents	120 Navy Pier
4 Foreword	132 Chicago Hotels
5 Introduction	136 Museum of Science and Industry
8 Chicago River	137 Chicago History Museum
16 Wacker Drive	138 Field Museum
22 Michigan Avenue	140 Haymarket Square
24 Old Water Tower	141 Maxwell Street
26 *Chicago Tribune*	142 Lincoln Park
32 Michigan Avenue Looking North	143 Lincoln Park Zoo
33 Michigan Avenue Looking South	146 Garfield Park
34 Wrigley Building	148 Humboldt Park
38 Michigan Avenue Bridge	150 Douglas Park
40 Art Institute	151 Jackson Park
46 Chicago Aerial Views	152 Washington Park
50 Chicago Beaches – North	154 Chicago & Northwestern Station
52 Chicago Beaches – Downtown	155 Chicago Union Station
53 Chicago Beaches – South	156 Ogilvie Transportation Center
56 Chicago Board of Trade	158 State Street
58 Buckingham Fountain	164 Marshall Field & Company
62 World's Columbian Exposition	168 Chicago Theatre
64 Century of Progress	170 Palmer House
66 Chicago Churches	174 Loop Streets
70 Cook County Jail	182 LaSalle Street
72 City Hall and County Building	184 Dearborn Street
78 Chicago Civic Opera	186 Adams Street
80 Chicago Coliseum	190 South Shore Country Club
82 Elevated Trains	191 Shedd Aquarium
86 Chicago Public Library	194 The Adler Planetarium
87 *Chicago Daily News*	196 Sports Arenas
88 Edgewater Beach Hotel	200 Avenues
92 Lake Shore Drive	202 Chicago Airports
100 Gold Coast	204 Evanston/Northwestern University
102 Grant Park/Millennium Park	206 Hyde Park/University of Chicago
108 Chicago Harbors	208 Old Chicago Post Office
112 Marina City	

FOREWORD
by Lawrence Okrent

Picture postcards presented the wonders of the world in color at a time when black-and-white photography dominated print media and travel was a difficult and expensive proposition. Postcards encouraged and nurtured human contact and postcards imparted a lasting pictorial record of the places we visited (as well as the places we hoped to visit).

I began collecting postcard images of Chicago very early in my 45-year professional career. I was never very concerned about the condition of the cards or whether they had been used or not. I was, however, particularly fascinated with their graphic content. They ultimately became a valued part of a much larger pictorial archive of Chicago's development trajectory that I had the pleasure of assembling. All of this proved to be very useful in the course of my work, as the subject of prior condition is frequently relevant in the field of city planning and urban development.

The added bonus to my interest in Chicago *per se* was the sheer abundance of postcards with *Chicago* content. This made them inexpensive to acquire individually, and gloriously diverse in their subject matter, pictorial quality, printing technology, and chronology.

In the days before widespread use of the telephone, the penny postcard was the principal means of casual interpersonal communication. Shoeboxes all over the country filled with postcards with written messages on one side about the weather, family chit-chat, or news of safe arrival at the end of a long train ride; and on the reverse, to our good fortune (in many many cases) the wonders of Chicago— from the celebrated to the ordinary

The age of digital imagery has allowed us to preserve—and share—for all posterity the simple cardboard-backed pictures that constitute an enduring record of our cultural, technological and social history. I hope you enjoy this book as much I have enjoyed gathering and archiving the modest artifacts that constitute a significant part of its illustrative content.

Lawrence Okrent is president emeritus of Chicago-based Okrent/Kisiel Associates, which has provided professional consulting services in the fields of urban/ land planning and zoning since 1979. Mapping and aerial photography figure prominently in the firm's work. In 2017 Mr. Okrent contributed more than 27,000 of his aerial photographs (1985–2015), and 5,500 architectural photographs to the Special Collections Research Center at the University of Chicago. He is the author of *Chicago From the Sky: A Region Transformed*, published by Chicago's Neighborhoods, Inc., 2013.

INTRODUCTION
By Gary T. Johnson

(Mr. Johnson is the eighth President of the Chicago History Museum)

The mission of the **Chicago History Museum** is to "share Chicago's stories." At first glance, it might seem that the image in a photograph or on a postcard is not a story at all, just a frozen moment in time. In a book like this, one that masterfully curates images gathered over almost a century and a half, there are stories everywhere.

First, there is ***the long story***, the grand sweep of Chicago's history from the Great Chicago Fire of 1871 to the present, with downtown buildings and transportation as the particular focus. For 36 hours, the fire moved from just southwest of the downtown to the northeast, right through the center of the city. Nobody has the exact numbers, but at least 300 died and many others left town, never to return. 18,000 structures were destroyed, and approximately one-third of the city's 300,000 residents lost their homes. Chicago already had great civic pride before the fire, as the city's pre-fire geometric growth was greeted on America's East Coast with puzzlement and disbelief. The destruction of a modern city was a shock to the world, and so was the city's rapid rebuilding after the fire. With that background, starting over after the fire is the logical place to begin this long story, and the grand sweep of these images, with new buildings still replacing old buildings and new forms of transportation still replacing earlier ones, shows that this narrative continues today.

That's the long story, but every single image also offers ***a short story***. Why was it that someone captured this image at that moment of time? What was the photographer or the artist trying to tell people? Beyond the aesthetic qualities, there is the object — maybe a new building, or a scene — maybe State Street with a new look. The stories, of course, aren't always the new. As time went on and the city kept building and rebuilding, old buildings and nostalgic scenes sometimes would highlight the way the city used to be.

There is the ***moving picture story***, told with frames offered side-by-side to show developments. The authors here took particular care in offering a number of frames of the same view from different eras, images that illustrate a changing city.

Then there is the ***personal story***. Anyone who has lived in Chicago for any period of time, including new arrivals, will find photos that trigger personal thoughts. I visited the Loop as a child and worked in the Loop for 28 years So as pictures start appearing from the 1950s forward, countless personal stories come to mind.

There are the ***stories that answer questions***. This is especially true, I think, for individuals whose families have lived in Chicago for a long time. My Grandma Margaret used to say that her teen-age job of racing around downtown Chicago delivering the *Chicago Inter Ocean* newspaper were some of her favorite memories.

This was around 1910, so when I see images from that era, I recall her stories and I have a better idea of what she saw back then and why it all seemed so exciting to her. She once told me that the most dramatic moment in her life came when she was a young child and saw her first automobile. When I look at these images and see Chicago absolutely choked with traffic around that time, I can see why someone born in the horse-and-buggy era would find Chicago's downtown so exciting.

Let's not forget the **stories that leave you wanting more**. Consider the images of Navy Pier. It was built in 1916 for freight and passenger ships, served as a training center for the U.S. Navy during World War II, and then became the home of the University of Illinois at Chicago. After a period of underutilization, in 1995 it was redesigned as a public attraction, and now it is being redesigned again. As this book is being written, the Chicago Shakespeare Theater is about to open a new theater space at Navy Pier— "the Yard." Where will this story go next?! Then, of course, there are the transportation stories. One of the strengths of this collection is the depiction of so many forms of transportation — boats, buses, streetcars, and various types of rail. Particularly fascinating are the forms of transportation that are no longer here, such as the Green Hornet streetcar, and means of transportation in places where you no longer find them, such as large ships docked in the Chicago River, back when what is now Wacker Drive was the city's main harbor.

The images themselves have a story. A little-known fact was that Chicago was one of the postcard-producing capitals of the world. *(Chalk up another accolade for Chicago!)* Some of the postcards in this book were made by the Curt Teich & Company, which was in business from 1898 to 1978.

This was the world's largest printer of view and advertising postcards, and the company operated in the North Side of Chicago from its plant near N. Ravenswood and W. Irving Park. (The Newberry Library has the largest collection of cards made by Curt Teich.) Another creator of postcards was Barnes & Crosby, many of whose glass negatives and master photographs are in the collection of the Chicago History Museum. From 1897, Barnes & Crosby operated from its studio in downtown Chicago, and many of its most iconic photographs and photographic engravings depict buildings and scenes from the Loop.

Chicago also is where techniques for photographing skyscrapers were developed. Two photographers, Ken Hedrich and Henry Blessing were approached by Chicago architects at the end of the 1920s with the thought that more could be done by photographers to do justice to the architects' creative work. The Hedrich Blessing firm was in business from 1929 through 2017 and led that effort. (The Chicago History Museum owns the Hedrich Blessing Archive.)

Let me conclude with an appreciation of the work of photographer and co-author Steven Dahlman. The on-going story of a changing Chicago would not be complete without the work of contemporary photographs. Dahlman's work is in the tradition of those who created the earlier images in this book and stands up to their level of excellence. It is particularly illuminating when his photos depict a place that was captured in the past.

The story of a changing Chicago is an open-ended one. This book is particularly valuable because it takes the story right up to the present chapter.

CHICAGO RIVER

The Chicago River is part of a complex system of waterways, much of which is manmade, including the North Shore Channel, the Sanitary and Ship Canal, and the Cal-Sag Canal. The river originally flowed into Lake Michigan, but this caused frequent pollution of the lake. The Chicago Sanitary District was created in response. Between 1895 and 1900, the river was re-engineered, reversing the flow of the main channel and South Branch away from the lake and into the Illinois River watershed.

WACKER DRIVE

Wacker Drive, originally proposed in Daniel Burnham's 1909 *Plan of Chicago,* follows the south bank of the main channel and east bank of the South Branch of the Chicago River.

The original intent of the two-level design was to create a formal traffic artery at the upper level while allowing for the delivery of river-borne freight to fronting properties at the lower level.

MICHIGAN AVENUE

Also imagined in the Burnham plan, Michigan Avenue replaced the much narrower Lincoln Parkway and Pine Street. The Michigan Avenue bridge, completed in 1921, became the easternmost crossing of the river until the bridge at Lake Shore Drive opened in 1937. The Avenue from the Michigan Avenue/DuSable bridge north to Oak Street was dubbed "the Magnificent Mile" by real estate magnate Arthur Rubloff.

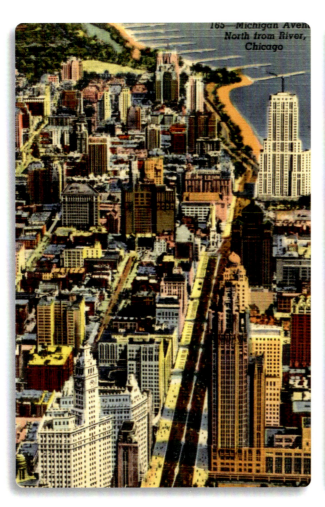

OLD WATER TOWER

From Oak Street to the Chicago River, North Michigan Avenue is known as the Magnificent Mile. South Michigan Avenue extends from the DuSable/ Michigan Avenue Bridge to the city's South Side. The Mag Mile replaced the former Lincoln Parkway and Pine Street north of the Chicago River and today is one of the most famous streets in Chicago.

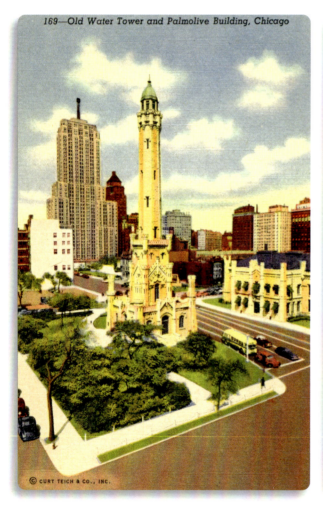

CHICAGO TRIBUNE

The iconic Tribune Tower was built in the 1920s based on the design of architects John Howells and Raymond Hood after a worldwide design competition, and is located on the east side of the Magnificent Mile at the Chicago River. The self-proclaimed "World's Greatest Newspaper," (and owner of *WGN* broadcast media) was founded in 1847 and rose to prominence under managing editor Joseph Medill. Perhaps its most famous editor, Colonel Robert R. McCormick, transformed it into a conservative publishing giant. The Tribune company owned the Chicago Cubs from 1981 to 2009.

MICHIGAN AVENUE BRIDGE, CHICAGO

A contemporary view looking north from inside the McCormick Tribune Bridgehouse and Chicago River Museum in the former southwest tower of the Michigan Avenue Bridge.

MICHIGAN AVENUE LOOKING NORTH

Michigan Avenue after dark. The Wrigley Building was illuminated at night beginning in 1921 and the Lindbergh Beacon atop the Palmolive Building was installed in 1930. (Photographer-Unknown. Courtesy of the Chicago Historical Society ICHi 52305).

MICHIGAN AVENUE LOOKING SOUTH

WRIGLEY BUILDING

The Wrigley Building on the city's Magnificent Mile along the Chicago River is located just west of Tribune Tower and north of the DuSable/Michigan Avenue Bridge. The site was personally selected by chewing gum magnate William Wrigley for his company's new headquarters. The twin towers were designed by architects Graham, Anderson, Probst & White. The south tower was completed in 1921 and the north tower in 1925.

MICHIGAN AVENUE BRIDGE

Looking south towards Wacker Drive and London Guarantee Building. (Courtesy of the Chicago Transit Authority).

ART INSTITUTE OF CHICAGO

Completed in 1893 to coincide with the World's Columbian Exposition, the original museum building was designed by the Boston firm of Sheply, Rutan & Coolidge. It has been expanded several times since. The Modern Wing, designed by Renzo Piano and completed in 2006, is the most recent.

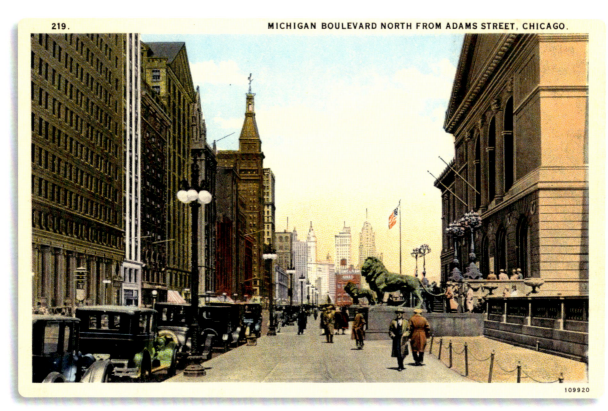

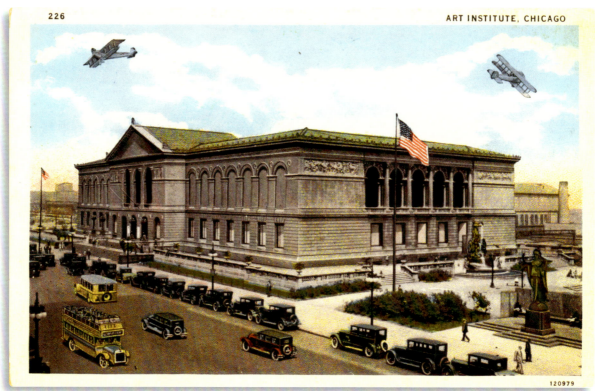

41

CHICAGO AERIAL VIEWS

CHICAGO BEACHES

Because the prevailing winds over Lake Michigan flow from the west, Chicago has no natural beaches. The city's beaches are largely manmade. All but four miles of the city's 28 mile-long shoreline are improved with public parks and beaches.

Chicago Beaches — North
In the city's far north side neighborhood of Rogers Park a series of small beaches are located at the east ends of several east-west residential streets. Sam Leone-Loyola Beach Park extends eight blocks south from Touhy Avenue to North Shore Avenue. From Thorndale Avenue south to North Avenue, a distance of nearly six miles, is a continuous band of beaches (Foster, Montrose, North Avenue) and parks along the lakefront.

CHICAGO BEACHES

Chicago Beaches–Downtown
The main Gold Coast/Near North beaches are at Oak Street, across from the famous Drake Hotel, and the Ohio Street Beach, just north of Navy Pier.

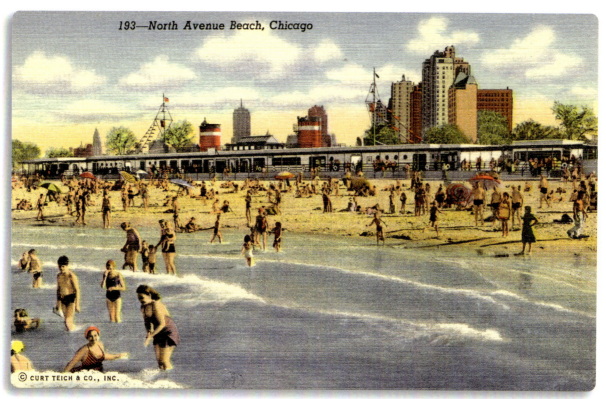

Chicago Beaches–South
The northernmost of the south side beaches is at 12th Street, just south of the Adler Planetarium. Additional beaches are at 31st Street, Oakwood/41st Street, Hyde Park/57th Street, Jackson Park, Rainbow Park (75th Street) and Calumet Park (100th Street). The infamous race riot of 1919 began at Rainbow Beach.

Jackson Park Pavilion Shelter, 57th Street and Lake in Jackson Park. (Courtesy of the Chicago Historical Society).

CHICAGO BOARD OF TRADE

Since its founding in 1848, the Chicago Board of Trade has been located at the foot of LaSalle Street. The current Board of Trade Building, designed by Holabird & Root and completed in 1930 was once—at 45-stories—the city's tallest. The building it replaced, designed by W. W. Boyington, was completed in 1885.

BUCKINGHAM FOUNTAIN

Dedicated in 1927 and named in honor of Clarence Buckingham, the brother of Kate Buckingham who donated the fountain to the city, it is one of the largest in the world and the centerpiece of Grant Park's formal layout.

World's Columbian Exposition, Agricultural Building, 1893. (Courtesy of the Chicago Historical Society, ICHi-23347).

WORLD'S COLUMBIAN EXPOSITION (1893)

Constructed in Jackson Park, the fair ran from May 1 to October 20, 1893 as a celebration of the 400th anniversary of Christopher Columbus's landfall in the New World. The master plan was prepared by Daniel Burnham, who went on to create the 1909 *Plan of Chicago*. Many architects and engineers participated in the project, including Louis Sullivan, whose Transportation Building is generally regarded as the fair's most significant. More than 27 million people attended the exhibition.

CENTURY OF PROGRESS

The Century of Progress was a world's fair held in Chicago in 1933 and 1934 to celebrate the city's centennial. The fairgrounds surrounded present day Burnham Harbor, with important exhibits on Northerly Island. Nearly all of the fair site was reclaimed from Lake Michigan and would later be used for the Merrill C. Meigs Field Airport and McCormick Place. The theme of was technological innovation. It proved to be a big success with more than 40 million attendees over its two-year run.

CHICAGO CHURCHES

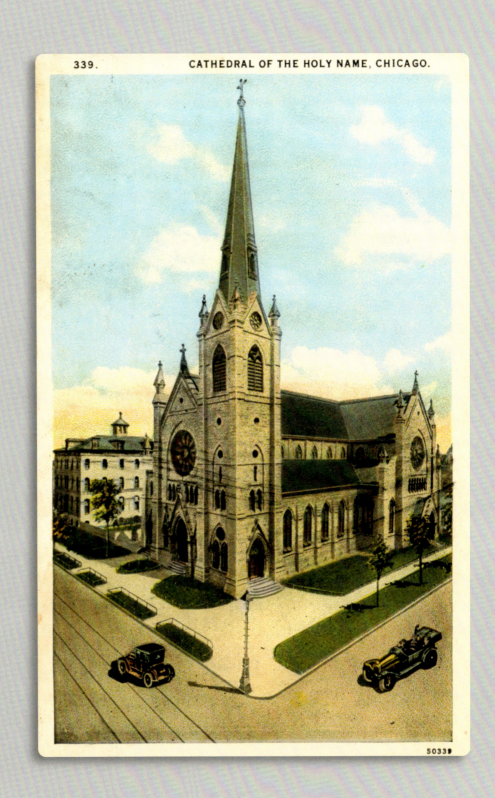

CHICAGO CHURCHES

COOK COUNTY JAIL

The old courthouse and jail at 54 W. Hubbard Street opened in 1850. It was in this building in 1875 that President Lincoln's widow was found to be incompetent.

A second Cook County prison, The Bridewell, was built in 1852 at Polk and Wells. The present Cook County prison and criminal court complex at 26th Street and California Avenue dates from 1871, and has been expanded several times, most recently in 1995. It is the largest single jail site (96 acres) in the United States.

CITY HALL AND COUNTY BUILDING

There have been seven Chicago City Halls and County Buildings on the same site since the city was incorporated in 1837.

The current city hall-county building, completed in 1911, was designed by Holabird & Roche. Its immediate predecessors were the County Building of 1881-1882 designed by James J. Egan and Alex Kirkland, and the City Hall of 1884–1885, designed by John M. Van Osdel.

CHICAGO CIVIC OPERA

The Civic Opera House was the first modern office building constructed on the north-south segment of Wacker Drive. It opened on November 4, 1929, and was designed by the architecture firm of Graham, Anderson, Probst & White. Its $23 million cost was funded partly by industrialist Samuel Insull and partly by opera subscribers who bought stock in the development entity. The venture went bankrupt in 1932. The Lyric Opera Company of Chicago was established in 1954.

CHICAGO COLISEUM

Chicago has had several large indoor arenas prior to the construction of the United Center in 1994, including the third Chicago Coliseum at Wabash Avenue/15th street (demolished 1982), the International Amphitheater at Halsted St./42nd St. (1934–1999) and the Chicago Stadium at Madison/Wood St. (1929–1994). All served as venues for sporting events, exhibitions, and numerous national political conventions.

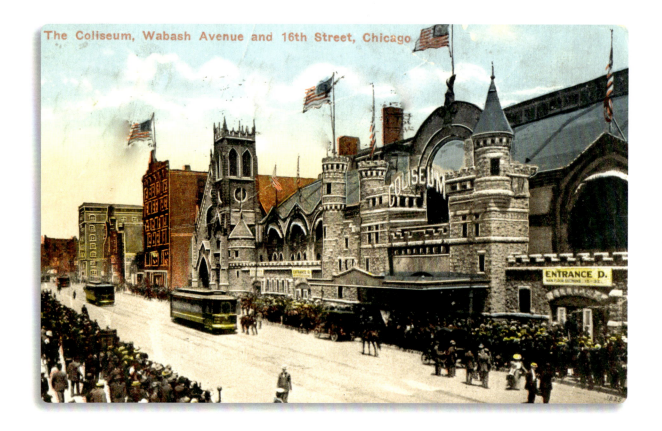

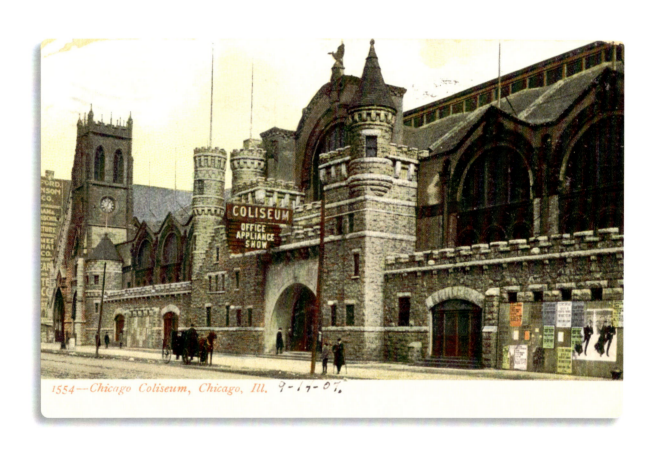

ELEVATED TRAINS

The first "L" began operations in 1892 on the South Side. The Lake Street Elevated was inaugurated in 1893. Construction of the Union Loop in 1897, and the addition of the North Side line in 1900 resulted in a unified system. The State Street Subway opened in 1943. In 1947, the Chicago Transit Authority was created from the combined assets of the Chicago Rapid Transit Company and the Chicago Surface Lines.

CHICAGO PUBLIC LIBRARY

Chicago had no public library prior to the Great Chicago Fire of 1871. The first public library was established by the Chicago City Council in 1872, when 8,000 books were donated to the city in the name of Queen Victoria. It was located on the site of the present day Rookery Building at LaSalle and Adams. The Chicago Cultural Center at Michigan and Randolph housed the library from 1897 to 1975. After occupying two temporary locations, the library moved to the Harold Washington Library Center in 1991. The new building was designed by Hammond, Beeby & Babka, winners of a highly-publicized design competition.

CHICAGO DAILY NEWS

The *Chicago Daily News* was founded in 1875 by Melville E. Stone. Under the subsequent leadership of Victor Lawson it introduced advancements in classified advertising and syndication of news stories, and offered a first-class foreign news service. In 1929, it moved to a new headquarters at 400 W. Madison Street on the South Branch of the Chicago River. The *News* ceased publication on March 4, 1978. The building is now known as Riverside Plaza.

199—Daily News Building, Chicago

EDGEWATER BEACH HOTEL

The famous resort hotel located in the Edgewater neighborhood of the city's Far North Side was designed by Benjamin H. Marshall and Charles F. Fox and first opened in 1916. A second hotel building was added in 1924; and in 1928 an apartment tower completed the ensemble. The hotel was best known for its private beach on Lake Michigan, its boardwalk and restaurants, and its on-site radio broadcasts.

Edgewater Beach Hotel, ca. 1920. (Photographer-unknown. Courtesy of the Chicago Historical Society, ICHi-16101).

LAKE SHORE DRIVE

Lake Shore Drive was built in segments along Lake Michigan beginning in the 1880s. The first section opened in front of Potter Palmer's long demolished "Castle" (1350 N. LSD) in the neighborhood that became known as the Gold Coast. The Drive now extends for over 26 miles from the South Shore community on the city's South Side, north past downtown, and ends at Hollywood Boulevard in the Edgewater neighborhood on Chicago's Far North Side.

Pedestrians on lakefront walkway in Lincoln Park with excursion boats in background, ca. 1910. (Photographer-Casey Prunchunas. Courtesy of the Chicago Historical Society, ICHi-62335).

Lake Shore Drive and N. Michigan Avenue, looking east. (Photograph by Lawrence Okrent, Okrent Associates)

GOLD COAST

GRANT PARK | MILLENNIUM PARK

Grant Park was created almost entirely from landfill. The area between Michigan Avenue and the Illinois Central tracks was filled largely from the debris of the Great Fire of 1871. The area east of the tracks was filled between 1897 and 1907 using material dredged from the lake and construction spoils. The park was protected from commercial development due to a series of lawsuits initiated by Montgomery Ward who wanted the park space along Lake Michigan to be "forever open, clear and free." Later, the 24-acre Millennium Park was constructed largely over an open Illinois Central rail yard from Randolph Street to Monroe. It officially opened in July, 2004, and has become one of the most popular attractions in the city.

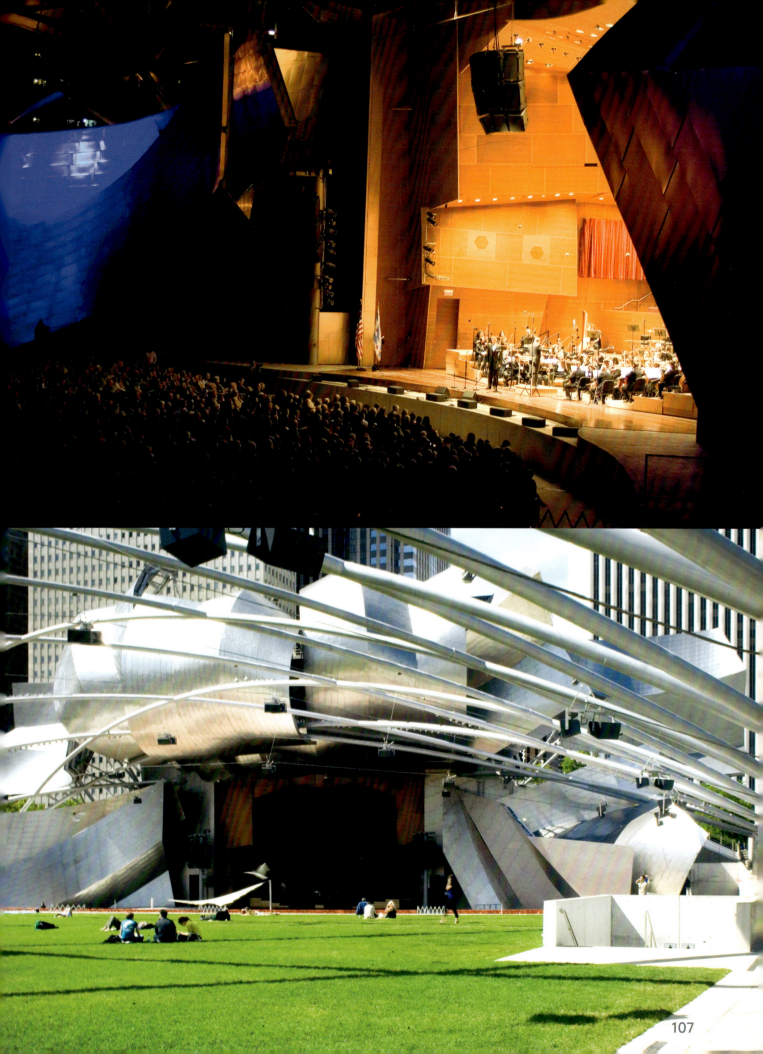

CHICAGO HARBORS

Chicago boasts a large system of municipal harbors along Lake Michigan that are operated by the Chicago Park District for over 6,000 recreational boaters. These include Montrose Harbor, Belmont Harbor, Diversey Harbor, DuSable Harbor, Monroe Harbor, Burnham Harbor, 31st Street Harbor, 59th Street Harbor, and the Jackson Park Inner and Outer Harbors. There is also the Chicago Harbor located at the mouth of the Chicago River.

MARINA CITY

Designed by architect Bertrand Goldberg and built between 1960 and 1968, as a mixed-use residential and commercial building complex, Marina City is located along the north bank of the Chicago River. It was the first building in the United States to be constructed using tower cranes. It is a "city within a city" with numerous onsite amenities including restaurants, a live music venue, bowling alley, grocery store and a marina.

Chicago's Marina City Twin Towers

MERCHANDISE MART

Opened in 1931, the Merchandise Mart was designed by Graham, Anderson Probst & White architects and built by Marshall Field & Company along the Chicago River between Orleans and Wells Street on the city's Near North Side. It is the world's largest building and contains more than four million square feet of floor space. Originally the space was used for showrooms and manufacturing facilities for Marshall Field & Company.

NAVY PIER

Municipal Pier (its original name) was constructed in 1913–1916, under the authority of the Chicago Harbor and Subway Commission, to provide dock and shed space for lake-borne freight. Only the eastern tip was originally dedicated for recreation and public access. It was renamed Navy Pier in 1927 to honor World War I veterans. The US Navy used it as a training center during World War II. From 1946 to 1965 it served as the campus of the University of Illinois Chicago campus. The current iteration of the pier as a tourist destination came to fruition in 1995.

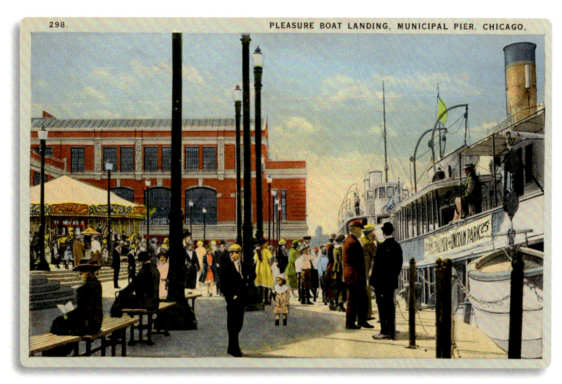

Photographer: Nick Ulivieri
(Courtesy of Navy Pier, Inc.)

(Courtesy of Navy Pier, Inc.)

Photographer: Heidi Zeiger
(Courtesy of Navy Pier, Inc)

(Courtesy of Navy Pier, Inc.)

CHICAGO HOTELS

MUSEUM OF SCIENCE AND INDUSTRY

Originally the Palace of Fine Arts at the 1893 World's Columbian Exposition in Jackson Park, the building was in disrepair when, in the 1920s, philanthropist Julius Rosenwald decided to financially support its renovation and improvement. The museum first opened in the 1930s as the Field Museum and then was known as the Rosenwald Museum before becoming more popularly known today as the Museum of Science and Industry. The Museum is 350,000 square feet, and houses over 2,000 exhibits including a replica of a coal mine and the Henry Crown Space Center. A captured World War submarine, the U-505 was moved to a new enclosure inside the museum in 2005.

CHICAGO HISTORY MUSEUM

Originally known as the Chicago Historical Society when it was established in 1856, the first museum building was destroyed by the Great Chicago Fire of 1871. A second was destroyed by fire in 1874. A fireproof building designed by Henry Ives Cobb was later constructed at 632 N. Dearborn in 1896. The museum moved to its current facility at 1602 N. Clark St. in 1932. The building has been enlarged since then, in 1972, and again in 1988.

THE FIELD MUSEUM

The Field Columbian Museum was first established in the Fine Arts Building of the Columbian Exhibition. As the original building was not built to be a permanent structure, its accelerating decay and the museum's growing collection compelled the museum to seek a new facility. The current museum was constructed over a period of five years, beginning in 1916, on riparian land reclaimed from Lake Michigan, The permanent collection includes more than 20 million objects.

HAYMARKET SQUARE

The Haymarket was originally an open air farmers market. It is almost universally known as the location of the Haymarket Square Riot of May 4, 1886. The incident began when a group of anarchist activists protested the death of workers during a labor strike elsewhere in the city. When spectators gathered to listen to speakers, police arrived to break up the demonstration. A bomb killed seven of the officers. Following the event, there were arrests, trials, and several of the activists were sentenced to death. Ultimately, four anarchists were executed. A commemorative statue honoring the dead officers was unveiled at the site in 1889. After being repeatedly vandalized in the 1960's and 1970's, the statue was relocated to Chicago police Headquarters, where it was most recently rededicated in 2007.

MAXWELL STREET

Located in a small area of the lower Near West Side a neighborhood that attracted many impoverished immigrants to Chicago from Eastern Europe, Maxwell Street became a thriving open air flea market for generations of Chicagoans. Urban renewal ultimately led to the market's demise. The construction of the new campus of the University of Illinois, first implemented in 1965, was the beginning of the end, although informal commerce continued on an ever decreasing scale thereafter.

LINCOLN PARK

Originally the city's main cemetery, the land and adjacent shoreline were acquired by the city in 1864. Graves were subsequently moved to other cemeteries and the first phase of park development, from North Avenue to Fullerton Avenue, began. Lincoln Park was named for the 16th President of the United States after his assassination. By the end of the 19th Century, the park included fountains, statuary, walkways, a conservatory, a bicycle path, and a zoo. Today Lincoln Park extends along the lakefront all the way from North Avenue to Thorndale.

LINCOLN PARK ZOO

Begun in 1868 with a pair of swans given to the city by New York's Central Park, the zoo expanded rapidly to include a lion house, primate house, and other large buildings. It became famous in the 1950s when zoo director Marlin Perkins hosted the television show *Wild Kingdom*. It is the only free zoo located in an American city.

Sea Lion pond at Lincoln Park Zoo, 1889. (Photographer-Unknown. Courtesy of the Chicago Historical Society, ICHi-62339).

GARFIELD PARK

One of the three large parks in the West Side Park System, Garfield Park was laid out by William Le Baron Jenney in 1870. When Jens Jensen became chief landscape architect for the West Park District, the planting program was completely renovated. The Garfield Park Conservatory designed by Hitchings and Company of New York was added in 1905–1907.

HUMBOLDT PARK

The park originated in the 1860s on the city's Northwest Side near North and California Avenues. In the 1870s, architect William Le Baron Jenney created a landscape plan that included lagoons and plazas. Later, landscape architect Jens Jensen added a formal rose garden and an additional lagoon in the western section of the park.

DOUGLAS PARK

Located on the city's West Side in the North Lawndale community, Douglas Park was named for U.S. Senator Stephen A. Douglas. Dedicated in 1869 and designed by William Le Baron Jenney, the park was part of the West Park System that also included Garfield and Humboldt Parks. The facilities included an outdoor gymnasium, swimming pool, and natatorium.

DOUGLAS MONUMENT, 35TH ST. AND THE LAKE, CHICAGO, ILL.

PERGOLA AND LILY POND, DOUGLAS PARK, CHICAGO

JACKSON PARK

Jackson Park extends from 57th Street to 67th Street, along the shore of Lake Michigan. The city's third largest park was designed by Frederick Law Olmsted, who also served as the landscape architect for the World's Columbian Exhibition, which was held in the park in 1893. The Fine Arts Building for the fair was reconstructed as the Museum of Science and Industry, and opened in 1933 during the Century of Progress exhibition.

302. "THE REPUBLIC" STATUE IN JACKSON PARK, CHICAGO.

161:—Lake in Jackson Park, Chicago, Ill.

WASHINGTON PARK

Planned and designed by landscape architects Frederick Law Olmsted and Calvert Vaux in 1871, Washington Park extends over an area of 372 acres. Although located in the Washington Park/Woodlawn neighborhood, its eastern boundary abuts Hyde Park and the medical campus of the University of Chicago. The park's characteristic features include an arboretum, gymnasium, and sports fields, as well as the celebrated Lerado Taft sculpture, *The Fountain of Time*.

CHICAGO AND NORTHWESTERN RAILWAY STATION

Originally constructed in 1881 on Wells Street north of the river, the terminal was demolished to make way for the Merchandise Mart. The rail company built a new station at Madison and Canal Streets in 1911. In 1984, the second station was replaced by the 42-story Citicorp Center, although the new project was designed to sustain ongoing commuter rail operations.

159—Dearborn Street Station, Chicago

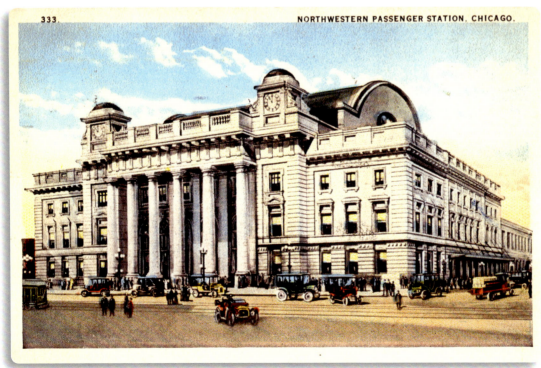

333. NORTHWESTERN PASSENGER STATION, CHICAGO.

CHICAGO UNION STATION

The first Union Station was built in 1879–80 at Canal and Monroe Streets. At peak, five different railroad companies used it as a passenger terminal. The second Union Station, located between the Chicago River and Clinton Street, south of Adams St. opened in 1925. The vast Great Hall, 110-feet in height, is capped by a barrel-vaulted skylight.

OGILVIE TRANSPORTATION CENTER

STATE STREET

Originally called the Vincennes Trail, State Street became known as Hubbard's Trail (for Gurdon Saltonstall Hubbard) and was next known as State Road. In its early days the road was unpaved and muddy. However, in the late 1860s, businessman Potter Palmer bought up much of the fronting property, transformed it into State Street, and convinced Marshall Field and Levi Leiter to move their dry goods stores from Lake Street and open a department store called Field, Leiter & Co. For most of the twentieth Century, State Street would become the city's world-class shopping and movie palace destination. The corner of State and Madison once "The world's busiest" is the point of origin for the Chicago street numbering system.

735. State Street South of Lake, Chicago.

State Street looking North from Madison Street, Chicago.

316. BUSIEST CORNER IN THE WORLD, STATE STREET, LOOKING NORTH FROM MADISON STREET, CHICAGO.

MARSHALL FIELD AND COMPANY

Marshall Field and Levi Leiter established their department store on State Street in 1867, but it was destroyed by the Great Chicago Fire of 1871 (and replaced in 1873). Field bought out Leiter in 1881. A new building designed by Daniel Burnham opened in 1893. In 1897, Field installed the Great Clock at the corner of State and Washington Streets and the phrase "meet me under the clock," entered the city's lexicon. Throughout the 20th Century, Marshall Field & Company was the premier shopping destination on State Street. Marshall Field's name vanished from State Street in 2006 when Macy's acquired the company's assets.

CHICAGO THEATRE

Originally called the Balaban and Katz Chicago Theater when it opened in 1921 on State Street between Randolph and Lake Streets, the building was the flagship of the B&K group of theaters. A movie "palace" in a most literal sense, it was designed by Cornelius and George Rapp. Hosting both movies and live stage shows the theater has a seating capacity of 3,800.

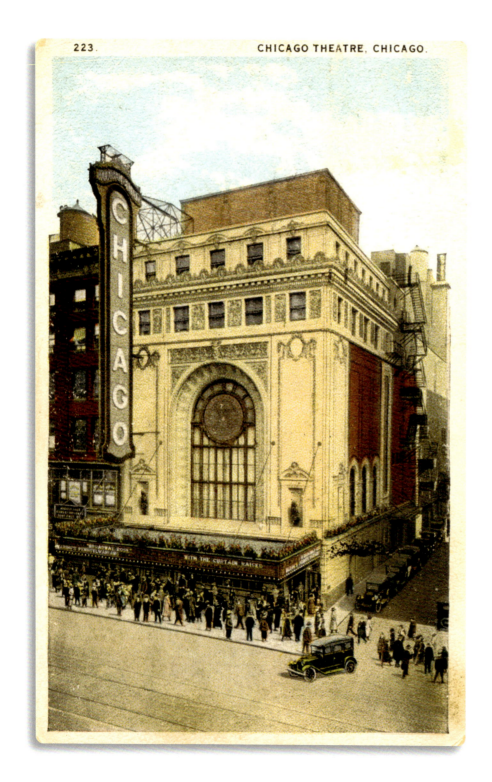

PALMER HOUSE

The first Palmer House Hotel opened at State and Monroe Streets in September, 1870. Originally developed by Potter Palmer, who was responsible for State Street's becoming the city's most iconic street, that original hotel building was destroyed in the Great Chicago Fire of 1871. Today's Palmer House is the third to occupy the site. Designed by Holabird & Roche, it was completed in 1925 and became part of the Hilton chain in 1945. It is now known as the Palmer House Hilton

PALMER HOUSE, CHICAGO.

Ladies entrance to the Palmer House Hotel, 1903. (Photograph by *Chicago Daily News*. Courtesy of the Chicago Historical Society, DN 0001231).

LOOP STREETS

5449. WABASH AVE., NORTH FROM MONROE, CHICAGO.

682. Washington St., East from Dearborn St., Chicago.

These 1913-era steel "L" cars, viewed at Wabash and Lake, were built with center doors that were not used. (William C. Hoffman photo, Wien-Criss Archive).

Adams Street looking east towards Dearborn. The familiar Berghoff Restaurant sign is visible in the background. (Courtesy of the Chicago Transit Authority).

The bus-only lane on Washington Street looking west from the "L" at Wabash. (Courtesy of the Chicago Transit Authority).

LOOP STREETS

214. STATE AND MADISON STS., "BUSIEST CORNER" IN THE WORLD, CHICAGO.

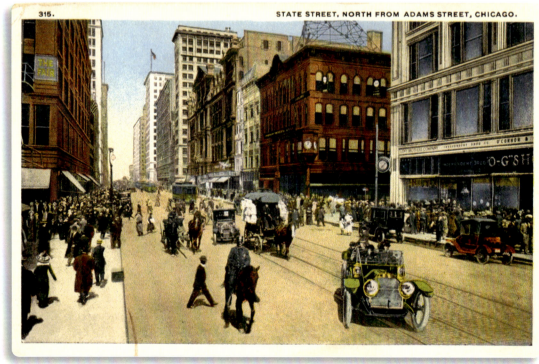

315. STATE STREET, NORTH FROM ADAMS STREET, CHICAGO.

State and Randolph Sts.
Chicago.

Madison St.,
looking East from Fifth Ave.,
Chicago.

Randolph looking west from State in 1933. (Courtesy of the Chicago Transit Authority).

Randolph Street looking east from LaSalle. (Courtesy of the Chicago Transit Authority).

LASALLE STREET

29 La Salle St. No. from Jackson Blvd., Chicago, Ill.

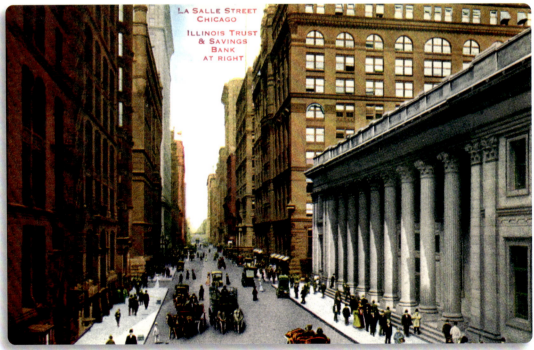

La Salle Street Chicago

Illinois Trust & Savings Bank at right

DEARBORN STREET

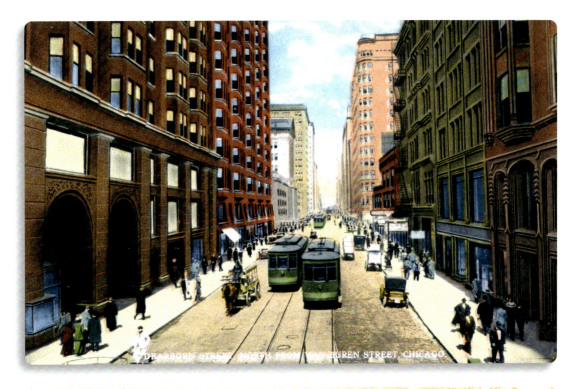

ADAMS STREET

Adams Street, Looking East from State, Chicago, Ill.

Adams Street looking east from Franklin. At right is the Marshall Field & Co. wholesale warehouse. (Courtesy of the Chicago Transit Authority).

SOUTH SHORE COUNTRY CLUB

The Country Club, designed by architects Marshall and Fox, opened in the South Shore neighborhood along Lake Michigan in 1905. It included a theater, stables, golf course, tennis courts, bowling green and private beach. Although membership was long restricted to white Christians, declining membership in the 1970's opened the possibility that racial and religious minorities might be admitted; but this did not happen. The club was sold to the Chicago Park District in 1975, and became the South Shore Cultural Center.

SHEDD AQUARIUM

The world's largest indoor aquarium opened on the Lake Michigan shoreline in 1929 and was named for John G. Shedd, the second president of Marshall Field and Company, who donated $2 million toward its construction. In 1991 the aquarium was expanded with the opening of the Oceanarium, designed by architect Dirk Lohan.

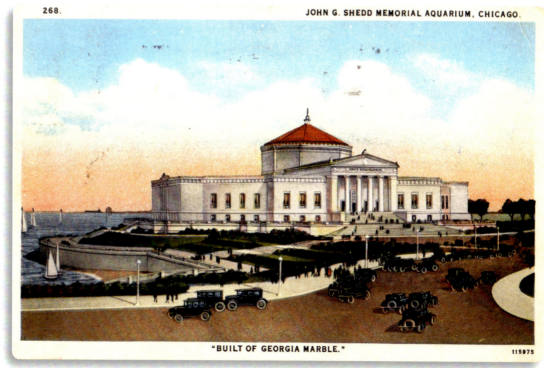

THE ADLER PLANETARIUM

The Adler Planetarium was conceived in 1928 by Max Adler, a retired executive with Sears Roebuck & Company, and brother-in-law of Julius Rosenwald. It opened in 1930 as the first modern planetarium in the Western hemisphere. Declared a National Historic Landmark in 1987, a complementary addition designed by Dirk Lohan was completed in 1999 to house several new exhibits, including the 60,000 square foot Sky Pavilion.

SPORTS ARENAS

The Chicago Stadium was the home of the Chicago Blackhawks from 1929 until 1994, and the Chicago Bulls from 1967 to 1994, when it was demolished. Both teams now play their home games at the United Center. The Stadium hosted the Democratic National Conventions of 1932, 1940 and 1944, and the Republican National Conventions of 1932 and 1944.

Comiskey Park The long time home of the Chicago White Sox was named for Charles A. Comiskey, the team's owner from 1900 until 1931. It was located on the north side of 35th Street at Shields Avenue, immediately north of the team's current home, Guaranteed Rate Field. Since the park opened in 1910, four years after their 1906 World Series victory over the Cubs, the White Sox won only one World Series during their occupancy of Comiskey, in 1917.

Soldier Field
Located on the Near South Side lakefront, just south of the Museum Campus, the first iteration of Soldier Field opened in 1924. The name was adopted on November 11, 1925 as a memorial to US soldiers killed in combat. In its original configuration it had a seating capacity in excess of 100,000. It has been the home field of the Chicago Bears since 1971. The stadium's interior was extensively reconstructed and modernized in 2002–3. The seating capacity of the reconfigured Soldier Field is 61,500.

WRIGLEY FIELD

Built in 1914 for the Chicago Whales of the short-lived Federal league, Wrigley Field has been the home stadium for the Chicago Cubs since 1916. It has experienced numerous updates over the years, including the planting of ivy along the outfield walls in the 1930s, and the introduction of lights and night baseball games in 1988. It was also the Chicago Bears' home field from 1921 to 1970. Today, it is undergoing another major modernization by the new owners, the Ricketts family. In 2016, the team won its first World Series since 1908—and its first in Wrigley Field.

AVENUES

Sheridan Road, looking North from Wilson Ave., Chicago.

Garfield Park, looking east on Jackson Blvd., Chicago.
One of the large West side parks, area 187 acres.

CHICAGO AIRPORTS

Midway Airport
Midway Airport opened in 1927 on the city's Southwest Side as Chicago Municipal Airport. By 1932, it had become the World's Busiest. In 1949, it was renamed Midway Airport to commemorate the pivotal World War II battle in the Pacific Ocean. Midway Airport served more than 11 million passengers in 2016.

O'Hare Airport
In 1946, the City of Chicago purchased over a thousand acres northwest of the city, and, in 1955, transformed the pre-existing Orchard Field Airport (ORD) into O'Hare International Airport. It was renamed 1949 in honor of War II flying ace, Billy "Butch" O'Hare. In total number of takeoffs and landings O'Hare surpassed Midway Airport by 1961. In 2016 O'Hare handled more than 875,000 flights and served more than 37,500,000 passengers.

EVANSTON | NORTHWESTERN UNIVERSITY

First settled in the 1830s, the town was named for John Evans, one of the founders of what became Northwestern University in 1853. Evanston, incorporated in 1863, is the first suburban municipality located along Lake Michigan on Chicago's northernmost boundary. The town grew outward from its central core at Fountain Square. Open land remained on the Chicago-Evanston border as late as the eve of World War I.

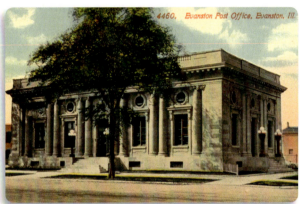

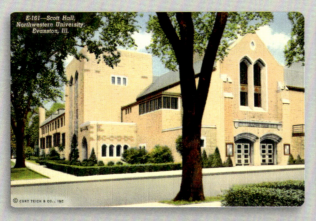

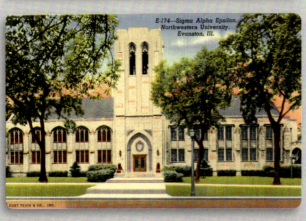

HYDE PARK | UNIVERSITY OF CHICAGO

The University of Chicago was established in 1890, with John D. Rockefeller its principal benefactor. William Rainey Harper was its first president. The U of C is considered to be one of the premier private universities in the country. Over the years its faculty has included more than 90 Nobel laureates. The world's first man-made self-sustaining nuclear reaction took place December 2, 1942 beneath the stands of Stagg Field, by then a defunct football stadium. The site was named a National Historic Landmark on February 18, 1965.

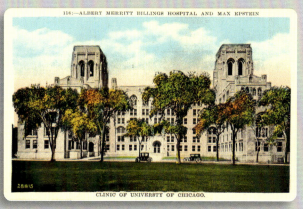

OLD CHICAGO POST OFFICE

When constructed in 1922, a passageway was left in the base of the building in anticipation of the construction of what was to become the Eisenhower Expressway, which did not happen for another 25 years The vast nine-story building, designed by Graham, Anderson, Probst & White was originally needed to handle the enormous volume of mail-order business generated by Montgomery Ward and Sears, Roebuck and Company. The structure in Art Deco style was expanded in 1932 to 2.5 million square feet of space. After the new main post office south of Harrison opened in 1997, the old post office ceased operations. property was sold in 2016 to a development company which intends to convert it to office use, with rooftop parking and a river walk.